$9.95

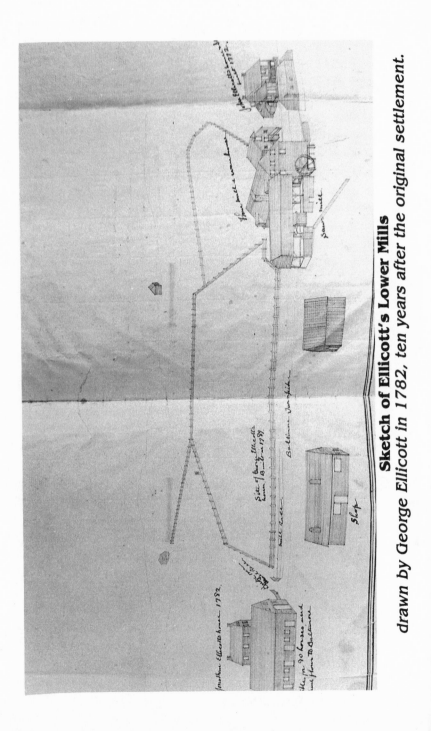

Sketch of Ellicott's Lower Mills

drawn by George Ellicott in 1782, ten years after the original settlement.

This is dedicated to my grandmother, Margaret Mylander.

Ellicott Mills

The Ellicotts:
Striving for a Holy Community

Alison Ellicott Mylander

Historic Ellicott City, Inc.
Ellicott City, Maryland

Published by
Historic Ellicott City, Inc.
Ellicott City, Maryland

Design and Composition by
Clover Typography, Inc.
Silver Spring, Maryland

Printing by
Spectra Press, Inc.
Columbia, Maryland

Manufactured in the United States of America
First Edition
1991

ISBN No.: 0-9631792-0-9

FOREWORD

The Ellicott family, an influential Quaker family living in Maryland during the late eighteenth and early nineteenth centuries, seemed remarkable in several ways. When compared to neighboring contemporary families, this family was atypical in several respects: scientific, restless, affectionate, and commercially enterprising.

In addition to their puzzling differences, the Ellicotts were of personal interest. My grandmother, Margaret Mylander, was an Ellicott descendant. Although she passed away several years ago, her influence has endured through the impact she had upon her family and friends. More than any other person, she served as my mentor. I respected her abilities, interests, and integrity. To me, this study has been both a tribute to her and an attempt to understand my family better.

I analyzed various aspects of the Ellicott family's story during the late eighteenth century and first half of the nineteenth century. First, I addressed areas typically examined in any family study. These topics included religious background, education of children, and public involvement.

Second, I focused upon family relationships. Although a great deal had been written recounting the public accomplishments of the men in the Ellicott family, little had been written describing the Ellicott women or the private side of life in the Ellicott family. With this focus in mind, I sought clues to explain differences in actions and attitudes between this Quaker family and contemporary American families. Fortunately, the Ellicotts' correspondence, homes, inventories, and wills provided glimpses into their relationships and attitudes toward family members.

Third, I studied the effect religion had upon their lives. The Ellicotts' story may answer some general questions regarding Quaker families during this period. For example, their commercial enterprises posed a common question about the motivations of economically comfortable Quakers.

The results of my study depicted the Ellicotts as different from contemporary families. While not being perfectly representative of typical American families during this period, the Ellicott family did typify many Quaker families.

The author would like to thank Professor Cindy Aron of the University of Virginia and Chris Carpenter for their comments and encouragement. Also, this work would never have been published without the support of Virginia Kinney and other members of Historic Ellicott City, Inc.

PHOTO CREDITS

John L. Clark
Mrs. Henry M. Fitzhugh
Ms. Joetta Kram
Mr. Herbert H. Johl
The Howard County Historical Society
The Oella Company

Table of Contents

CHAPTER I
A New Beginning

In 1772, three brothers, Joseph, Andrew, and John Ellicott, moved their families from Bucks County, Pennsylvania to an uninhabited area on the outskirts of Baltimore, Maryland. These brothers and their descendants established Ellicott Mills, now Ellicott City. Here, they became innovators in a variety of business, agricultural, and community endeavors which earned them reputations as early American men of science and as public servants.

The Ellicotts endured hardships to reach their purchase of four miles of land along the Patapsco River. Along with their wagons, carts, wheelbarrows, drafthorses, household goods, and agricultural implements, they travelled across land and water.[1] Dreams of creating a new mill community inspired them to undergo this arduous journey. The three orphaned brothers had already built and managed a highly successful mill in Pennsylvania. Suffused with ambition, they hoped this venture would be as successful.

The Ellicotts began construction immediately after arriving. They built a large, log boarding house with many apartments to accommodate the mechanics and laborers that had accompanied them. Next, they constructed a saw mill to prepare the wood for the homes.[2] Using the abundant granite available, they soon added a school and a courthouse.[3]

In addition to beginning a town, the Ellicotts also had a tremendous impact on Baltimore area's productivity.[4] They persuaded many Baltimore landholders to fertilize their soil and to produce wheat rather than tobacco. If they had not, many families would have

John Ellicott's House & Store,
built 1772.

moved out of the area. Tobacco planting had exhausted the soil; families, like the Dorseys, Clarks, Hammonds, and others, had planned to leave.[5] They, like Charles Carroll, complained about dwindling cash revenues as the value of tobacco land fell.[6] The Ellicotts, after having tested the soil, urged their new neighbors to try different methods to restore soil productivity. More important, the brothers realized that the Maryland climate and soil were better suited for wheat than for tobacco. To entice their neighboring farmers to switch crops, the Ellicotts offered to build roads and to process their neighbors' first wheat harvest free of cost.[7] Carroll, one of the signers of the Declaration of Independence, was the first to switch his crop to wheat. His large profit quickly convinced other farmers.

The crop switch increased earnings and helped maintain the soil.[8] Earning a fair profit, these farmers decided to remain and helped to bolster a once declining economy. This economic change transformed the environment; an atmosphere of security and growth replaced one of despair, insecurity, and decline.

Shortly after completing a road to Frederick, Ellicott and Company next constructed a store. The store sold "articles of fine quality," including linens, silks, satins, tea sets, groceries, and mathematical instruments brought from New York, Philadelphia, and London, "at a fair rate of prices." With such attractions, the store became quite popular:

> For a long series of years the store was a place of resort for all the influential men for miles around, who came to sell their grain, to make purchases, to receive their letters and papers from the post-office, which was opened in one of its rooms, or to discuss political, legal, or scientific questions.[9]

According to one description of the store, its visitors enjoyed "the fine abilities and character of the Ellicotts: men who were not only well read on all such subjects, but who combined therewith courteous manners,

3

Friends Meeting House & Grave Yard

earnestness in pursuit of knowledge, and becoming gravity."[10]

The Ellicotts also built a Friends Meetinghouse. After travelling twice a week for several years to the Elkridge Meetinghouse, the Ellicotts built one in 1800.[11] This building, placed on the highest point in their town, symbolized the importance of the Quaker religion in their lives.

As the years passed, the number of buildings increased and several of these buildings conveyed the Ellicotts' emphasis upon the family, education, enterprise, and religion. Eventually, the Ellicotts brought their dream to fruition: a healthy and growing community emerged along the banks and hills surrounding the Patapsco River.

Footnotes

[1] Harry Lee Hoffman, Jr. and Charlotte Feast Hoffman, *American Family History: Fox, Ellicott, Evans* (Cockeysville, Maryland: Fox, Ellicott, Evans Fund, 1976), p. 37.

[2] Ibid., p. 1A.

[3] In fact, the Ellicott family frequently donated land and stone to build various churches when residents of Ellicott Mills requested them, even though the family did not share the same religious beliefs.

[4] Celia M. Holland, *Ellicott City, Maryland: Mill Town, U.S.A.* (Tuxedo, Maryland: Printers II, Inc., 1970), p. 3.

[5] Ibid.

[6] Francis Stein, *Howard County History* (Baltimore, Maryland: Howard County Historical Society, 1974). p. 97.

[7] By the harvest of 1774, the Ellicotts had built a mill "one hundred feet long and of proportionate breadth and height, with spacious chambers for the storage of grain. . . (which) contained machinery combining all of the prominent inventions of Joseph, Andrew, and John Ellicott, and was ready to manufacture the finest wheat flour." Hoffman, p. 37.

[8] Holland, p. 3.

[9] Hoffman, p. 39.

[10] Ibid.

[11] Ibid., p. 38.

Ellicotts Upper Mills,
built by Joseph Ellicott 1775

CHAPTER II
The Quaker Religion

Quaker principles helped to explain many of the Ellicotts' actions. Fortunately, a number of Quaker documents exist to reveal Quaker attitudes about the family and to describe what was considered the proper, or ideal, behavior of members.

According to Quaker historian Frederick B. Tolles, "Quaker thinking on most subjects varied relatively little from place to place, so that the ideas of English and American Friends down at least to the Revolution can be regarded as practically interchangeable."[1] Although great distances separated some Quakers, travelling ministers and constant exchange of tracts and spiritual biographies maintained close contact between Quakers. For the most part, the collected evidence of the Ellicotts' actions and behavior supported this, since they coincided with the experiences and behavior of other American Quakers.

The contrast of eighteenth and nineteenth century Quakerism with Puritanism highlighted noteworthy similarities and differences. In many ways, Quakers shared more with Puritans and other Protestants than they differed from them. Nevertheless, the comparison illustrated the Quaker religion and explained several of the Ellicotts' "peculiarities."

I

Like many Protestant sects, Quakerism was a lay religion with no professional religious leaders or paid clergy.[2] Instead of paid ministers, anyone who felt inspired during the service spoke.

The Quaker and Puritan views of original sin contrasted starkly. Unlike the Puritans who believed people were born sinners, the Quakers believed people were born innocent, but sinned inevitably. Because they were born stainless from corruption, they felt optimistic and thankful to God. This gratitude to God fueled their self-confidence.

Just as individuals controlled their decision to sin or not, individuals also controlled their capacity to do good works and to earn salvation. While Puritans believed in predestination, Quakers transferred much of the responsibility for actions to the individual.[3] Every person determined his or her own fate. Any Quaker individual had the capacity to recognize his or her spiritual illumination and to live a life which led to salvation, if he or she chose.

For Quakers, an inward light became the guiding force and the avenue of religious experience. Quakers emphasized spiritual illumination, in addition to the ethical teachings of Christ. This inward Christ, not the historical Christ followed by the Puritans, became preeminent. William Penn described "that of God" which guided Quakers: "For they were directed to the Light of Jesus Christ Within them, as the Seed and Leaven of the Kingdom of God . . . a faithful and True Witness, and just Monitor in every Bosom."[4] For this reason, Quakers subordinated the Bible, scriptures, and other historical texts to their feelings.

The Quaker attitude of Christian personal sacrifice also differed from the Puritan attitude. Quaker self-denial revealed the subservience of physical things to the spiritual.[5] In contrast, Puritan self-denial was a form of abstinence rooted in a fear of the individual's predestined grace. By comparison, Quaker actions, believed to be divinely guided, exuded confidence. According to Quakers, God, working in individuals, could produce sinless acts. Theoretically, individuals could even attain perfection. This self-assurance and conviction seemed less evident in other Protestant sects, although the outward manifestations sometimes resembled each other. For example, both Puritans and Quakers often worked hard and succeeded financially; an uncertainty and a desire to show their grace motivated Puritans, while God's direction and goodness guided the Quakers.

The Quakers' internal experiences and literal interpretation of the Bible allowed them to lead good, simple Christian lives.[6] Authority figures, elders in the church, and parents maintained order and discipline to unify meetings and the community. In addition, all members could assist by acting as their brothers' keepers, just as in Puritan communities.[7] Any discipline, however, lacked punitive actions; brothers and sisters merely advised each other.[8] Members might have imposed social, economic, or familial pressure upon each other to achieve their religious aims, but they did not impose religious sanctions. Although Quaker parents, as well as brethren and sisters in the meetinghouse, wanted to direct and to encourage people to lead good lives, religion and salvation remained internal affairs which did not require external proof.[9]

II

Quakers considered their community to be an extended family. The family metaphor and familial references exhibited Quaker unity, particularly within the meetinghouse. Members of this large family had spiritual authority over children, just as the immediate family did. Often, many parental figures and observers may have been a nuisance, but at times they also proved advantageous. A caring body, such as a meetinghouse, insured against disasters — be they economic misfortunes or death-related.[10]

Because the child's development could extinguish his or her innocence, members and parents watched carefully to prevent any signs of evil and to encourage any seed of light.[11] Members had confidence that children were born innocent and remained so until they had the

11

capacity to comprehend the difference between good and evil; therefore, Quakers neither baptised infants nor doubted their salvation.[12]

In order to nurture the child's spiritual growth and to ensure the survival of the Quaker religion, Quakers, like Puritans, hoped to provide a proper environment and education for their youth. Both religions faced a dilemma: they both wanted a congregation of saints. The Puritans created a Halfway Covenant in the 1660's for members' children to profess their faith. By this covenant, the children could attend services in their youth. At maturity, they had to convince the congregation that they had undergone a conversion experience and had been saved. On the other hand, Quaker children became full members at birth and need not face this examination.[13] Therefore, Quakers, like other religious groups, needed to insulate their children from worldly temptations to hope to maintain a meetinghouse of saints.

Parents had primary responsibility for children. They "(took) heed to themselves" to provide sterling examples of simplicity and moderation.[14] In 1800, the Baltimore Yearly Meeting of the Society of Friends urged parents "to bring up those under their direction in true plainness and moderation, and to the more frequent reading of the Scriptures of Truth, endeavoring to restrain them from reading pernicious publications."[15] The following year, the Baltimore Monthly Meeting reminded parents "in all respects. . . to walk before (children), that their minds may be convinced of the sure rewards of Peace for well doing."[16] Parents hoped to provide examples and guidance within a blend of tenderness and discipline.[17] During these formative years, they wanted to instill patience, self-control, and humility in children.

The dictates of the meetinghouse pervaded virtually every aspect of childhood. Both with their immediate family at home and with their larger family at the meeting and school, a religious atmosphere surrounded children and committed them to Quaker lifestyles early.[18]

III

Often, Quakers established their own schools attempting to guarantee their childrens' insulation from evil influences and to immerse them in a controlled religious environment. From 1750 until the turn of the century, the Quaker population and area determined educational facilities and availability.[19] In particular, Pennsylvania and New Jersey made great efforts to provide instruction for children. In some of these schools, "the pupils were not all Friends, and charity was administered to children of any religious denomination."[20] During the nineteenth century, Quakers continued to recognize education's critical importance and gave it much attention.

More than most contemporary schools, Quaker schools stressed useful knowledge. Since "education" was "the stamp parents gave their young," William Penn did not want children burdened with "Words and Rules: to know Grammar and Rhetorick, and a strange Tongue or two, while his natural Genius to Mechanical and Physical or natural Knowledge" lay fallow.[21] Quaker education emphasized "concrete and material things, of actually expending energy in the pursuit of truth."[22] Thus, modern science and the Quakers shared a combination of empiricism and rationalism.[23]

In fact, Quaker historian Frederick B. Tolles explained that scientific studies sometimes became recreation for Quakers and for Puritans. Sometimes, these pursuits eradicated desires for more licentious activities:

> The high standard of personal morality which the Quakers set for themselves kept them away from the playhouse, the ballroom, the gambling den, and the bull pit. Scientific study as an avocation had the virtues of being useful, of exercising the mental powers, and, by revealing God's plan in a natural world, of promoting a reverent frame of mind.[24]

Quakers encouraged useful study and experiments because the practical world wore "the mark of its maker."[25]

By knowing Him better through His works, experimentation and careful study could lead the inquirer closer to God.

Generally, children began these schools at the age of six, seven, or eight — after they had mastered their letters and were fit to study.[26] At these schools, children did not receive grades and could terminate their studies when they were ready to leave.[27] Often, the sexes were separated, particularly during the nineteenth century. Education of young ladies rarely extended beyond reading and writing.[28] While women may have been viewed as spiritual equals, Quaker men were not yet ready to consider them intellectual equals.[29]

After completing their education at the age of fourteen, most young men and women apprenticed or trained in some skill until they married. During this period of critical importance, parents and neighbors surveyed carefully for moral transgression. The Baltimore Monthly Meeting hoped "by thus watching over one another for good, friends in their different allotments may speak a word in season to the weak, that by being united together in the faith, the Church may come forward out of the several weaknesses which are apparent."[30] During these formative years, adults, brethren, and sisters provided many examples of proper adult behavior and gave advice on every issue. In fact, members of the meeting actively participated even in the selection of one's mate.

IV

Quakers believed only God could bring people together in marriage. They thought God, not physical attraction or wealth, originated a holy desire. Quakers posited that love existed between people before marriage, if God formed a bond of their inward lights.[31] Thinking religion sanctioned their love, they avoided the Puritan fear of devotion to a person detracting from devotion to God.[32] However, this religious bond of love could only exist between spiritual equals, so the meeting

14

forbade members to marry outside of the church. Marriage between Quakers preserved the religion and upheld religious ideals in the family.[33]

The meeting, as well as the parents, discussed marital unions and granted permission. The couple underwent a formal procedure to request permission:

> (They) first appeared at the women's meeting, and a female friend introduced them to the men's meeting. There they declared that 'with the Lord's permission and friends approbation they intend to take each other in marriage.'[34]

Next, the betrothed needed to furnish both parents' verbal or written approval, regardless of their ages. Afterward, they attended the next monthly meeting to announce again their intention to marry and to hear any objections. Finally, the couple married at the next meeting in the presence of the members.[35] This lengthy procedure imposed control and required patience, even in the passion of romantic love. Furthermore, it displayed and strengthened the familial bond between members; the members formed and consecrated the bond of marriage.

V

In all of these ways, the Quaker religion attempted to shape members and future members. By stipulating the proper behavior for families, schools, meetings, and even the marriage procedure, the meetinghouse created an environment conducive to leading a good, Christian life. Quaker communities hoped to insulate members and to remove temptations as much as possible. In addition, notions of youthful innocence and of romantic love before marriage helped Quakers to accept early nineteenth-century sentimentalization and glorification of youth and marriage.

Quakers created a strong sense of community. By referring to each other as family members, they shared much of their lives and fostered a sense of unity among one another. Together, they strove to live by three principles: equality, simplicity, and peace.[36]

Footnotes

[1]J. William Frost, *The Quaker Family in Colonial America: A Portrait of the Society of Friends* (New York: St. Marten's Press, 1973), p. 5.

[2]Ibid., p. 3.

[3]Ibid., p. 14.

[4]Frederick B. Tolles, *Meetinghouse and Countinghouse: The Quaker Merchants of Colonial Philadelphia, 1682-1763.* (Chapel Hill: University of North Carolina Press, 1948), p. 4.

[5]Frost, p. 18.

[6]Ibid., p. 25.

[7]Ibid., pp. 52-3.

[8]Ibid., p. 59.

[9]Ibid., p. 25.

[10]Ibid., p. 65.

[11]Ibid., p. 66.

[12]Ibid., p. 67.

[13]Ibid., p. 68.

[14]Ibid., p. 76.

[15]Baltimore Yearly Meeting of Friends, 1800, Maryland Hall of Records.

[16]Ibid., 1801.

[17]Frost, p. 77.

[18]Ibid., p. 80.

[19]Ibid., p. 97.

[20]Ibid.

[21]Ibid., p. 94.

[22]Tolles, p. 207.

[23]Ibid., p. 206.

[24]Ibid., p. 209.

[25]Ibid., p. 211.

[26]Frost, p. 123.

[27]Ibid.

[28] Ibid., p. 127.
[29] Ibid.
[30] Baltimore Yearly Meeting, 1798.
[31] Frost, p. 152.
[32] Ibid.
[33] Ibid., p. 156.
[34] Tolles, p. 172.
[35] Ibid., p. 173.
[36] Ibid., p. 7.

CHAPTER III
Education: The Stamp Parents Give Their Young

The Ellicott family emphasized education. As Quakers, the family appreciated the importance of reading the Bible to nurture each individual's spiritual growth. Yet, the family members, both male and female, valued education and shared a sincere intellectual curiosity which seemed to extend beyond religious necessity.

The education of Ellicott children seemed atypical — particularly when viewed in historical context. In general, inadequacy and irregularity crippled colonial education, if local and familial conditions permitted it to exist at all. Mothers, older siblings, or poor widowed women often taught children. Unfortunately, most of these tutors lacked sufficient training themselves.[1]

Generally, most young boys attended grammar schools, where available. In these schools, the boys improved their reading and writing abilities and studied science, geography, history, and any languages taught. Since many colonial areas lacked adequate population or equipment to instruct formally, these outlying areas relied upon the free time and willingness of any educated adults in the area.

When education was available, most girls either faced neglect or received an education even more limited to the basic rudiments. The permissible amount of education assisted them in their domestic duties and enabled them to read the Bible or to write simple letters. Generally, additional education was feared; "excessive" education might "unsex" them. With this fear in mind, a popular English author cautioned women to shun the topics of

19

"politics, philosophy, mathematics, or metaphysics;" "they would render you unwomanly indeed (and) . . . would damp that vivacity, and destroy that disengaged ease and softness, which are the very essence of your graces."[2]

The American Revolution altered colonial women's expectations and perceptions of themselves dramatically. Many women found that war experiences instilled them with confidence and self-reliance, helping to displace their previous dependency.[3] Due to the shortage of local men during the war, women took on new work — inside and outside the family. In the process, they received sole responsibility of the family, as well as occupational and managerial training. These experiences suggested women's capabilities and heightened their desire to improve female education.

Republican ideology provided the language with which a few women writers expressed their grievances and demands. Couching their complaints in the rhetoric of the revolutionaries' fight, Judith Sargeant Murray and others gave American leaders unmistakable parallels between the women's demands for educational reform and the revolutionaries' demands for independence. In 1801, an "American Lady" demanded female access to knowledge to effect "women's emancipation from injustice and oppression."[4] Another female author employed a similar strategy in a *New York Magazine* article in 1794:

> Since the Americans have bravely established their liberties (notwithstanding the vain efforts of tyranny) we hope their modesty will keep them from exercising that despotism over us, which they so openly despised in their masters.[5]

In addition, the new republic needed well-educated, virtuous women for its very survival. According to the republican ideology, the virtue of society acted as the "basis of" and only hope for a fragile republic.[6] Only the vigilance of the citizens could preserve it. Historically, Whigs, like the Founding Fathers, purported republic governments to have failed because corrupt power eroded the citizen's liberties. Since the future of the nation depended on maintaining the character of its future citizens, the American leaders realized that households needed to become sources of virtue and stability. As manager and director of households, women received attention and an exalted role in society.[7] In *Liberty's Daughters,* historian Mary Beth Norton explained the exigency of having moral and educated women to protect the future of the nation:

> Because the nation would not survive unless its citizens were virtuous, and man's virtue was traditionally linked to woman's, it then followed that feminine influence would play a special role in the United States.[8]

Corrupt women doomed the future of the republic.

In addition to their impact upon American men, women shaped the future of society by raising children — the future electorate. Democracy necessitated the education and moral training of its youth. Just as the new ideology provided the basis for female educational reform, it prompted educational opportunities for children. Because the republic's success hinged upon the enlightenment of its electorate, education became a paramount concern. A proliferation of "academies" appeared after the revolution. These academies differed from the single teacher, short-lived boys' grammar schools and female adventure schools of the pre-revolutionary period.[9] The academies persisted longer and employed better qualified teachers. With permanent buildings, they could withstand difficult times. Also, additional teachers increased the teaching capacity of the school and the number of courses offered.[10]

Some of these academies instructed female students. As the new century progressed, Americans built more academies to provide education for women where it had not existed. In the few schools that already did educate both sexes, the sexes were separated. This separation manifested the emphases placed upon sexual differentiation, upon role differentiation, and upon the importance of protecting female morality. In 1809, Jacob Mordecai established the first female advanced school in Warrenton, North Carolina, and began a long tradition of separate female institutions of secondary education, or finishing schools.[11] By the early nineteenth century, the republic deemed female education a " 'duty' — a duty their parents owed them, a duty they owed themselves."[12] Rather than the colonial injunction for wealthy girls to be simply industrious, now they, like their brothers, were encouraged to improve.[13]

Although these schools separated the sexes and held a narrowly confined view of female education, at least they marked the beginning of secondary female education. Even if restricted in scope and limited to the wealthy, available female education signified a reassessment of the female role and an improvement.

I

Like most Quakers, the Ellicotts read sermons and spiritual tracts. They encouraged individual education so as to enable each member to read the Bible and to search for his or her "Inner Light," if for no other reason. They educated themselves, however, in other subjects as well.

For example, their library inventories listed a diverse selection of books including Atlases, cookbooks, scientific journals, and various novels, as well as Bibles. In fact, books accounted for up to ten percent of their total estimated household expenditures.[14] Compared to Jackson Turner Main's study of four hundred fifty-five Maryland estates between 1760 and 1776, these collections appeared unusually large. Main's study found only sixty-three percent of the estates to own any books at all, and one out of six of those with books had only a Bible.[15]

Respecting books and learning, the Ellicotts wasted no time in establishing a school for their children. Immediately after their arrival in the early 1770's and the completion of their residences, the Ellicotts built one:[16]

> A school was kept therein by the best teachers they could
> procure, and at a good salary, which was insured to them,
> whether the number of their pupils were large or small. .
> . all of suitable age were admitted irrespective of the
> means of their parents, and deficiency in this respect
> being supplied by the [Ellicotts].[17]

Since most contemporary schools educated only paying students, this early public school, open to all, seemed rare. This school may not have been the first public school in the Baltimore area, but it did provide an early example of a more egalitarian shift in attitudes towards education.

According to Martha Ellicott Tyson's description, the first school in Ellicott Mills resembled an academy more than it did either a boys' grammar school or a girls' adventure school. It had a permanent structure located east of the Patapsco River near the George Ellicott house.[18] This structure, as well as the Ellicotts' guarantee of the teachers' salary regardless of the number of pupils, ensured the school's continued existence, despite the possibility of a low attendance some years. In fact, this school educated children until 1834 and existed until 1868.[19] Different from its contemporary schools, this long-lasting school, boasting several teachers, resembled academies opened after the American Revolution.

Even more unusual, the school educated both boys and girls. Before the Revolution, girls rarely received an education in schools and, if they did, it was limited usually to domestic and religious spheres. Yet, the Ellicotts sent all of their children to school. In all likelihood, both sexes studied the same basic subjects. Martha Ellicott Tyson, Elizabeth Ellicott Lea, and Anne B. Ellicott probably received their education at this school.[20] Martha's and Elizabeth's publications and one of Anne's letters revealed that the women in the family were literate and probably well educated.

Even though the Ellicott boys and girls probably received the same education in school, their training differed outside of the classroom. References to male

Rock Hill College

apprenticeships provided the only early evidence of educational differentiation between the sexes. Fathers trained their sons for professions and in the sciences. As a boy of sixteen, Andrew, later the national surveyor, helped his father make a famous four-sided twenty-four tune musical clock.[21] Also, his brother George laid out the road between Baltimore and Frederick at the age of fifteen.[22] Not only were these remarkable educational opportunities, but they also suggested the trust and responsibilities given young Ellicott sons. There is no evidence the Ellicott girls received such training. More likely, mothers instructed them in the domestic arts. Mothers needed their daughters' assistance with heavy household tasks and time-consuming chores.

In the 1820's, however, the Ellicotts separated the sexes in school. The ostensible reason for this policy shift was "the increasing age and number of girls and boys," which "compelled a division of the school."[23] Maybe the Ellicotts' division marked their succumbing to attitudinal changes towards women — or, helping to create them. At this time, different attitudes emerged towards women, such as those described in a movement entitled The Cult of True Womanhood. These new attitudes encouraged sexual differentiation and separation; certainly, the Ellicotts' schools complied, at least. For whatever the reason, the Ellicotts established a new school and moved the boys to this different site.[24] In 1824, the boys moved again to what is now Rock Hill College.[25] Meanwhile, the girls remained in the increasingly cramped original school building. But the Ellicotts did not ignore the girls for long. In 1829, the Ellicotts donated property to the state of Maryland to establish the Patapsco Female Institute. Tradition had it that this impressive Greek building appeared "so classically beautiful of architecture, so unrivaled in impressive site, so picturesque in forest environment and background as to recall Hellenic monuments of beauty."[26]

This female seminary promoted "refinement of manners, delicacy, neatness, and health."[27] The school

Patapsco Female Institute,
built 1837, Mrs. Lincoln Phelps Principal.

boasted "good chemical and philosophical apparatus and a small geological and mineralogical cabinet."[28] Although courses ranged from Latin and French to American and universal history, the school structured the young girls' lives — even to the point of forbidding "miscellaneous books, newspapers or other periodicals without the consent of the principal."[29] Rather than stretch the young girls' minds too much, the seminary promoted needlework, the preparation of food, and intellectual interest in a few "proper" areas.

Nevertheless, the Ellicotts realized the importance of education and it remained central to their family lifestyle and child-rearing. Due to this appreciation of education, they established permanent, well-staffed schools before many contemporary Americans.

II

As adults, the Ellicotts continued their educational pursuits, particularly in the sciences. The Ellicott men established reputations as early inventors, clockmakers, surveyors, and astronomers. In fact, Andrew, the General Geographer of the United States and a member of the American Philosophical Association, was one of the very first American "men of science."[30]

Although the Ellicott men did not often patent their discoveries, their list of inventions is lengthy. They designed the wagon wheel brake and the use of lime (plaster) to restore soil productivity, to name a few of their discoveries.[31] After they encouraged wheat production rather than tobacco production in the Baltimore area, they created the grain elevator, an invention which revolutionized the mills. Most contemporary mills transported the wheat from one stage in the process to the next on the workers' — often slaves' — backs. The Ellicotts' grain elevator, or vertical mill, let the force of gravity move the wheat to the next stage. In addition to being a much more humane treatment of workers, this process proved more efficient and economical.

The Ellicott men's scientific interests, however, extended beyond commercial enterprises. To these men, scientific pursuits probably served as recreational hobbies, as well as profitable discoveries. Their pursuits constituted an intellectual exercise or a philosophical inquiry. A few "men of science," such as David Rittenhouse, Thomas Jefferson, and Benjamin Franklin, pursued such topics. These early recognized men of science were active members in the American Philosophical Association. Selected on January 20, 1786, Andrew Ellicott became one of the association's early members.[32]

Through this organization, Andrew became a fast friend of Rittenhouse, the Association's first president. Andrew spoke highly of Rittenhouse in several letters to his wife. He described his "valuable friend David Rittenhouse," whose birth was "one of those instances where strength of Genious independent of a liberal education or even the common advantages has raised himself a Monument of Fame more durable than all the glittering pomp attendant on Wealth and Power — Without Tutors and almost without the Aid of Books he mastered the most critical sublime parts of science."[33] Andrew's laudatory descriptions conveyed his appreciation of education, particularly a self-taught and practical education, over material comforts and power.

Andrew, the geographer, inherited his father Joseph's mathematical and scientific abilities, as well as his mechanical skills. Born in 1732, Joseph Ellicott was Andrew Ellicott's and Ann Bye's oldest and most gifted son.[34] He visited England in 1766 and there studied clock-making. In 1767, Joseph made a famous four-sided clock. Unlike any other in England or America, it measured the time of the year, the planetary orbits, the moon's rotation, and played twenty-four popular musical tunes.[35] By permitting his son to assist him with the construction of this clock, Joseph must have influenced and educated young Andrew (then sixteen). In addition, Joseph probably introduced his son to his friends, Thomas Jefferson and David Rittenhouse.

Andrew's uncle John Ellicott was supposedly the "first inventor of steamboats." Using propulsion, he sent a small boat down one of the mill-races.[36] While attempting to perfect the steamboat on Christmas Eve, 1790, he had an accident in which he lost his arm.[37] Without his right arm and at the repeated urgings of his friends and relatives, John "determined to abandon forever all further practical inquiry into the nature and power of the new element, and its adaptation to the wants and comforts of mankind." He was little surprised when he heard the news of Robert Fulton's success with the steamboat a few years later.[38]

Claiming these inventors and surveyors, the Ellicott family boasted several scientific men. Yet, they were not alone; some academically inquisitive Ellicott women shared this interest. Elizabeth Brooke Ellicott was one such woman. When her future husband George Ellicott courted her, his first gift to her was Ferguson's *Introduction to Astronomy*.[39] Also, Benjamin Banneker, the famous black scientist and a good friend of George's, gave Elizabeth one of his original almanacs.[40] Evidently, Elizabeth had a scientific curiosity to prompt such gifts. George's respect for Elizabeth's intellect and encouragement of her studies indicated that at least one of the Ellicott men recognized women's intellectual potential and encouraged their scientific interests — without fear that it would "unsex" them.

Thus, the Ellicotts appreciated education and respected intelligence. They developed their sons' and daughters' educational capabilities, particularly in religious pursuits and useful, scientific studies. In addition, these examples indicate that they chose spouses and friends with similar intellectual interests.

Footnotes

[1] Mary Beth Norton, *Liberty's Daughters* (Boston: Little, Brown and Company, 1980), p. 257.

[2] Ibid., p. 264.

[3] Ibid., pp. 265-73.

[4] Ibid., p. 270.

[5] Ibid.

[6] Ibid., p. 242.

[7] Ibid., p. 243.

[8] Ibid., pp. 243-4.

[9] In pre-revolutionary America, boys could attend private or public grammar schools and girls could attend adventure schools. Women of married couples taught the adventure schools, which were held in the women's or couple's home. "They were short-lived, with no staff other than the owners, and their course of study stressed ornamental accomplishments. By the 1760's, adventure schools teaching music, dancing, drawing and painting, fancy needlework, and handicrafts flourished." Ibid., p. 259.

[10] Ibid., p. 273.

[11] Ibid., p. 274.

[12] Ibid., p. 276.

[13] Ibid.

[14] Inventory analysis of author.

[15] Jackson Turner Main, *The Social Structure of Revolutionary America* (Princeton: Princeton University Press, 1965), pp. 254-5.

[16] Harry Lee Hoffman, Jr.. and Charlotte Feast Hoffman, *American Family History: Fox, Ellicott, Evans* (Cockeysville, Maryland: Fox, Ellicott, Evans Fund, 1976), p. 3A.

[17] Ibid.

[18] Celia M. Holland, *Ellicott City, Maryland: Mill Town, U.S.A.* (Tuxedo, Maryland: Printers II, Inc., 1970), p. 136.

[19] Ibid., p. 139.

[20] Martha Ellicott Tyson published several memoirs which include "The Settlement of Ellicott Mills" in 1865 and "A Sketch of the Life of Benjamin Banneker" in 1836 for the Maryland Historical Society. In addition, she was instrumental in the founding of Swarthmore College. Her sister, Elizabeth Ellicott Lea wrote *A Quaker Woman's Cookbook* which enjoyed considerable success. Its nineteen editions turned a large profit, permitting her to keep her two hundred acres. Also, Anne B. Ellicott sent a letter to her cousin Joseph Ellicott which survived among the "Lyman Spaulding Papers" at Syracuse University.

[21] Silvio A. Bedini, "Andrew Ellicott, Surveyor of the Wilderness," *Surveying and Mapping*, June 1976, p. 114.

[22] Phoebe Jackson, *Quaker Records* (Annapolis: Maryland Hall of Records, 1974).

[23] Holland, p. 137.

[24] Ibid.

[25] Ibid.

[26] Ibid., p. 139.

[27] *Heritage*, September 1986, 13:3.

[28] Ibid.

[29] Ibid.

[30] Silvio A. Bedini, Keeper of the Rare Books, Smithsonian Institution, personal letter, 10 October 1986.

[31] Hoffman, p. 3.

[32] Catharine Van Cortlandt Mathews, *Andrew Ellicott: His Life and Letters* (New York: The Grafton Press, 1908), pp. 55-7.

[33] Ibid., pp. 57-8.

[34] Ibid., p. 6.

[35] Ibid., pp. 8-9.

[36] Holland, p. 3.

[37] Hoffman, p. 152.

[38] Ibid.

[39] Silvio A. Bedini, *The Life of Benjamin Banneker* (New York: Charles Scribner's Sons, 1972), p. 73.

[40] Hoffman, p. 23A.

CHAPTER IV
Inspired Confidence

The Ellicotts encouraged everyone to learn and to speak one's mind. The meetinghouse created an environment conducive to individual thinking and to personal expression. The belief that God directed one's thoughts justified a firm sense of conviction in one's ideas. Speaking in the meetinghouse often preceded speaking in the town assembly. This confidence and willingness to suggest and to clamor for improvements led the Ellicotts and other Quakers to assume leadership positions.

Joseph, the eldest of the three brothers who moved to Maryland, served as High Sheriff of Bucks County, Pennsylvania, in 1768-9 and as a member of the Provincial Assembly.[1] He must have disagreed with most Pennsylvania Quakers who felt "that the present Situation of Public Affairs call(ed) upon (them) for services in a military Way, which from a Conviction of Judgment, after mature Deliberation, (they could) not comply with." By 1750, mounting revolutionary sentiment and numerous colonial riots placed public office responsibilities increasingly in conflict with the Quaker belief in pacificism; in an attempt to abide by their religion, many Quakers renounced Pennsylvania politics.[2] As High Sheriff, Joseph's duties probably required some decisions which had a military cast — exactly the type of decisions many other Quakers hoped to avoid.

The onset of the American Revolution created more opportunities for leadership — and for religious dilemmas. For peace advocating Quakers, it caused profound conflicts. An excerpt from the "Howard District Press" of 1847 stated that the Ellicotts' sentiments and prayers

33

supported the Revolutionary cause, despite their pacificism:

> they early espoused the cause of Independence in heart and soul. No Tory blood ran in the veins of a single Ellicott. Although they belonged to the peaceful Society of Friends, and were not expected to march to the bloody field, yet in all ways that a peaceful citizen can serve his country in time of war, they were ever among the foremost in the land.[5]

As the beginning of this testimonial suggested, the Ellicotts' Quaker background of oppression under English intolerance may have made them particularly sympathetic to the cause of freedom from Tory rule. Even though their religious beliefs prevented the Ellicotts from being military leaders, they still assisted the cause.

In fact, the revolution even led family members to question or to modify their attitudes toward the Quaker religion and some of its basic tenets. Joseph's son Andrew Ellicott probably exceeded other family members' patriotism. As a Major in General Washington's Elk Ridge Battalion, he, as did his father, "transgressed the principles of Friends to serve his country."[4] Born on January 24, 1754, Andrew was in his early twenties at the onset of the war. Many years later, he supported his decision to violate the Friends' advocacy of peace. In a heated discussion with Rittenhouse and Bishop Madison of Virginia, Andrew argued that the Friends' doctrine was wrong in regard to a defensive war. This reaffirmation of his actions show that his youthful transgression had not been just an impulsive decision.[5]

This transgression illustrated only one example of Andrew's transformation of Quaker ideals. He also questioned some Quaker outward manifestations, namely language and dress. He refused to use the "plain language" (thee and thou) or to date his letters First or Second Month.[6] Andrew was not alone. During the colonial period, new leadership, education, and economic liberties altered many Quakers' attitudes. Some Quakers began to question unnecessarily stringent religious restrictions and austerity. By 1776, the American Revolution forced numerous patriotic American Quakers to question pacifism; not only could a defensive war be justifiable, but the establishment of a nation resting upon virtue and equality of opportunities morally mandated it. By questioning some Quaker principles and outward manifestations, Andrew, like a faction of other Quakers, addressed changes of his time and represented certain divisions within his religion.

Despite Andrew's military duty, his greatest public benefits were not military ones. His greater contributions, like many of the contributions from his inventive family, were scientific. His inventions and surveying accomplishments proved helpful to both the public and the scientific community.

Using instruments he had developed, Andrew made weather predictions and printed them in a yearly almanac. He also included verse. In his almanac, "The United States Almanack(sic) for the Year of our Lord 1782; Being the Second after Leap Year, and the Sixth Year of American Independence," he reported an interesting tale from the Alleghany Philosopher. This Sage detailed the poor condition of "Mrs. Britain":

> Mrs. Britain, at this time, continues in a very low, lingering, languishing condition; . . . The disorder in her *bowls,* with which she has been for some years afflicted, gains ground; but she is most alarmed at the *inflamed* state of her *extreme parts;* and, indeed, . . . it is doubtful whether all of the cooling medicines prescribed by her ablest physicians will be able to prevent *amputations.* [7]

After descriptions of her debilitated "constitution" and her "dreadful distemper," the Sage explained that "she will be forced to acknowledge this year, in the fullest manner, the Independence of these United States."[8]

In addition to his almanacs and inventions, Andrew contributed as General Geographer of the United States. This appointment led Andrew to survey boundaries throughout the nation. He served his new country the majority of his adult life and helped to define both its boundaries and character. Historian Silvio A. Bedini delineated the crucial role the first American surveyors had to perform in our nation's history:

> After the war for independence . . . there was a growing demand for surveyors, and with the need for the definition of state and national boundaries, a greater degree of professionalism was required to eliminate existing, and to avoid future, conflicts.[9]

Without doubt, these men faced danger and inclement weather. In addition to these risks, they spent most of their time in uninhabited regions, away from their families and the comforts of civilization. According to Bedini, Andrew "was admirably suited to the role he was to play in the shaping of the new nation" and would "become one of the first American professionals." His natural scientific ability, health, large build, excellent scientific training, and dedication aided Andrew and helped him face dangers, such as bears, wolves, rattlesnakes, and Indians.[10]

He began his appointed surveying at the age of 30 in 1784 when he, with a distinguished group, completed the Mason-Dixon Line boundary and resolved disputes over its proper placement. Young Andrew, still relatively unknown, accompanied David Rittenhouse (America's first astronomer), Reverend John Ewing (Provost of the University of Pennsylvania), Thomas Hutchins, (then Geographer of the United States), Rev. James Madison (President of the College of William and Mary), Robert Andrews (a reputable public figure), and John Page (a later governor of Virginia).[11] For completing the task, the College of William and Mary recognized Andrew with an honorary degree of master of arts.[12]

During his surveying, Andrew demonstrated his expertise in the use and repair of scientific instruments. In his *Journal*, Andrew noted that some of his apparatus had been "so injured by transportation from one place to another through the wilderness, that if I had not been in the habit of constructing and making instruments for my own use, our business must have been several times suspended till the repair could have been made in Europe."[13]

Many of Andrew's male relatives shared his scientific interests. He frequently took his younger brothers, Joseph, Jr. and Benjamin, and his son, Andrew, with him. Through these trips, Joseph, Jr. acquired quite a reputation. After locating the western boundaries of the states of Pennsylvania and New York, as well as determining the United States-Canadian border with his brothers, Joseph received an appointment with the Holland Land Company. A treaty with the Indians, called the Holland Land Purchase, secured the nine counties comprising Northern Pennsylvania and Western New York. After surveying this territory, Joseph became the Holland Land Company's agent in January, 1800 — his fortieth birthday. His offer included a large salary, a grant of six thousand acres of land, and five per cent commission on all sales.[14] With all these enticements, Joseph moved permanently from Maryland to western New York. Here, he established the town of Batavia which later claimed many of his relatives.[15]

As the founder of this area, Joseph became a distinguished and respected leader, even on a national scale. In November, 1804, Joseph served as an Elector of the President and of the Vice-President of the United States.[16] Beyond this position, Joseph would not accept political positions; in fact, he refused his appointment of Chief Justice of Genesee County in 1803.[17] The motivation behind his refusal is no longer available and no plausible religious reasons appeared. Possibly, the responsibilities, the time commitment, or modesty deterred him.

Unlike Joseph, his brother Benjamin, another large landowner in western New York, actively sought political positions. Benjamin represented the district of western New York in Congress from December 7, 1817 to March 4, 1819. In 1821, Benjamin, nominated again to represent the region in Congress, lost to his Clintonian opponent, the incumbent Albert H. Tracy.[18]

37

Joseph Sr. and his sons followed a common trail among Quakers: the path from the meetinghouse to the townhouse. Other family members, like many Quakers, made public service contributions to their national communities in various reform movements.

I

American Revolutionary rhetoric and thought sparked revolutionary fervor in other areas. It is not surprising that Quakers — previously persecuted religious dissidents and proponents of personal freedom — became leaders in many of these.

Abolitionism became one of the most active movements. Many Quaker men and women, including the Grimke sisters and Lucretia Mott, worked in this area. Quakers banned slavery in the 1770's. Although nothing indicated that the Ellicott family members ever owned slaves in America, many of the Ellicott spouses and relatives through marriage manumitted large numbers of slaves in accordance with this decree.

In addition to the manumission of slaves, the Quaker religious beliefs enabled the Ellicotts to be early models, as well as leaders, in movements to improve educational opportunities for American blacks and for American Indians. Since the Quaker religion accepted and respected all individuals, believing the devout ones to be equal before God, the Ellicotts lacked some of the racial prejudices of other nineteenth-century Americans.

The Ellicotts' appreciation of intellect transcended contemporary racial separation. Joseph, Andrew, George, and Elizabeth (George's wife) befriended Benjamin Banneker, the famous black scientist. In fact, George first lent Banneker astronomy books and an astronomy table to teach him astronomy and, later, would check the computations in Banneker's almanacs before they were printed. Joseph taught Banneker to construct musical instruments and clocks. Andrew, by taking Banneker with him on several surveying projects and by presenting

Banneker to the American Philosophical Association, helped to make Banneker famous. Banneker's reputation spread quickly. More important, his accomplishments and intelligence brought many of the anti-abolitionists assumptions about black mental capacity into question.

The Ellicotts probably engaged in many abolitionist activities. Elisha Tyson, the famous philanthropist and abolitionist, married two of his four sons to Ellicott women. Elizabeth, Jonathan's and Sarah's daughter,

Elizabeth Ellicott Lea
(1793-1858)

married Elisha's second son, William Tyson on October 26, 1803 in an Ellicott Mills Friends Meeting.[19] Martha, George's and Elizabeth's daughter, married Nathaniel Tyson, Elisha's third son, on September 27, 1815.[20] Marital connections to abolitionists provided circumstantial evidence at best, but the marriages, coupled with the Ellicotts' involvement in all Friends' goals and projects, implied that the Ellicotts most likely became abolitionists.

Later, Martha wrote several memoirs, some of which the Maryland Historical Society published.[21] One of these was "A Sketch of the Life of Benjamin Banneker." Written in 1836, this account described Banneker's achievements, interests, and personality. Unfortunately, most information now available about Banneker is limited to

Martha Ellicott Tyson

this recount, because, as Banneker was buried, his house burst into flames (probably in 1804), and the fire consumed his numerous inventions.[22]

By the turn of the century, the Ellicotts provided a model of acceptance and friendship with an intelligent black man. Not allowing a difference in color to become a barrier, both the Ellicotts and Banneker respected each others' talents and enjoyed each others' company.[23]

II

When the Ellicotts arrived in Maryland in 1772, the area was wild and traversed only by Indians from nearby tribes. The Ellicotts not only maintained good relationships with these Indians, but they also fought for Indian education.

Shortly after the three Ellicott brothers first arrived, they established their first school in which neighboring children were welcome "irrespective of the means of their parents."[24] Two of the sons of Chickasaw chiefs attended this school.[25] Obviously, the Ellicotts permitted their sons and daughters to learn and to interact with these Indians.

The Ellicotts opened their home to Indian neighbors as well. Martha Ellicott Tyson's writings included an interesting description of several chiefs and their wives who stayed in her parents' home during Christmas week of 1807.[26] A curious girl of age twelve, Martha recalled their appearances, clothing, and conversations vividly. This visit brought Little Turtle and Rusheville, chiefs of the

Little Turtle

Miami nation; Beaver and Crow, of the Delawares; two Shawanese chiefs; and Marpau and Raven, chiefs of the Potowatomies who also brought their wives. Martha recounts Little Turtle's warm and appreciative introduction to Martha's mother, Elizabeth, and to the children. The mild manners and civilized dress of Little Turtle and of several other visitors contrasted with Marpau and Raven, who had a "warlike disposition" and whose "dress was entirely made up of the skins of wild animals, which had been killed by his own hand."[27] Raven's wife had yet another attitude; this "young and handsome woman, of a modest and downcast expression . . . did not seem to entertain the prejudices against civilized manufactures which existed in her husband's mind."[28] And she was not alone; one of the conversations between the family and its guests was a comparison between savage and civilized lives. Although Martha's description of this conversation between the Ellicott family members and these Indians was unclear, she did state that the Indians "favored civilization."[29]

Joseph Ellicott, in addition, had close Indian friends. Although most of the Ellicotts were later buried in the Ellicott Graveyard, Joseph's and several of his children's graves were interspersed between several Indian graves on his property in Upper Ellicott's Mills originally. Since the family gravesite would most likely have been shared with close friends, a strong bond of friendship probably existed between Joseph's family and these Indians.[30]

In addition to interacting with Indians, the Ellicotts worked hard on their behalf. The Friends of the Yearly Meeting in Baltimore sent the Ellicotts on missions to Washington, D.C., "to endeavor to improve the condition of the Indians by wise admonitions delivered to the different officials of the United States government."[31] Jonathan Ellicott, George Ellicott, Benjamin Ellicott, John Ellicott, and Elisha Tyson were cited as active men in Indian affairs.[32] On February 26, 1804, the Indian Committee urged George Ellicott, Gerard T. Hopkins (whose wife was George's wife's cousin), and Philip Denis to instruct the Indians in Fort Wayne, Indiana. They hoped an education in some useful knowledge, particularly agriculture, would improve their productivity, spark intellectual interests in other practical areas, and, in a broad sense, civilize them.[33]

Through various means, the Ellicotts assisted their new nation, defined its boundaries, and accepted and educated its downtrodden. Their contributions typified the efforts of many American Quakers during this time. The religion's emphasis on every individual's potential, on education, and on the organic community naturally attracted Quakers to political and reformist arenas.

Footnotes

[1]Catharine Van Cortlandt Mathews, *Andrew Ellicott: His Life and Letters* (New York: The Grafton Press, 1908), p. 7.

[2]Frederick B. Tolles, *Meetinghouse and Countinghouse; The Quaker Merchants of Colonial Philadelphia, 1682-1763* (Chapel Hill: University of North Carolina Press, 1948), p. 27.

[3]Mathews, p. 12.

[4]Ibid.

[5]Ibid., p. 13.

[6]Ibid., p. 12.

[7]Ibid., p. 14.

[8]Ibid., p. 15.

[9]Silvio A. Bedini, "Andrew Ellicott, Surveyor of the Wilderness," *Surveying and Mapping,* (June 1976): p. 113.

[10]Ibid., p. 119.

[11]Ibid., p. 116.

[12]Ibid.

[13]Ibid., p. 117.

[14]Hoffman, p. 168.

[15]Ibid., pp. 166-9.

[16]Ibid., p. 169.

[17]Ibid., p. 33A.

[18]Ibid., p. 179.

[19]Ibid., p. 42.

[20]Ibid., pp. 70-3.
[21]Ibid., p. 70.
[22]Ibid., p. 25A.
[23]Ibid., p. 60.
[24]Ibid., p. 3A.
[25]Holland, p. 136.
[26]Hoffman, p. 70.
[27]Ibid.
[28]Ibid.
[29]Ibid., p. 71.
[30]*Baltimore Sun*, Vertical File, Maryland Room, Enoch Pratt Library.
[31]Hoffman, p. 66.
[32]Ibid.
[33]Ibid., pp. 66-8.

Court House,
built 1843.

CHAPTER V
Within These Walls

Some American historians have recently described most late eighteenth-century marriages as instrumental, functional unions, based upon economic motivations more than upon romantic love. These historians attempted to determine a family's "modernity" by examining the evidence of affection between family members. Thus, one gage for studying the Ellicotts' modernity compared to contemporary families may be the presence of affection in their correspondence.

Late eighteenth-century family letters revealed considerable affection between Ellicott spouses. Take, for example, letters from Joseph to his wife Judith. Separated by a trip to London in 1767, Joseph claimed that his dear wife and children rarely left his thoughts, "so that he did not enjoy the hurly-burly and confusion of the great metropolis."[1] According to their niece Martha Ellicott Tyson many years later, Judith reciprocated his love and "never ceased to lament" his death until her own death in 1809.[2] Joseph's son Andrew also wrote affectionate letters to his wife Sarah. As General Geographer of the United States, Andrew spent long periods away from his family.[3] During his work, he spent "many waking Hours" "in the dead of Night, anticipating (his) return to (Sarah's) Arms, and once more enjoy the Charm of (her) Mind and Conversation."[4] He missed her sorely, since "every day til (his return was) as long as a month spent" with Sarah.[5]

Not only did Andrew and Sarah love each other, but they also loved their children. Eighteenth-century parents, according to historian Nancy Cott, generally viewed children with unsentimental, instrumental attitudes. In her study of eighteenth-century Massachusett's divorce cases,

Cott found that the petitioners displayed minimal and chiefly financial responsibility for their children.[6] But, Andrew's hundreds of letters to Sarah revealed emotional, intimate feelings towards his children. Without any doubt, Andrew loved and missed both his wife and children. His letters elaborated:

> Meet me in the road . . . a meeting that would be more joyful to me than the Greatest Estate, or most Superb Title this country can bestow. (Since) nothing but Sleep draws my reflections from you, and our little Babes; and my constant prayer that you, and they, enjoy the Health which I do, and that such a long separation may never again take place.[7]

In fact, every one of his letters inquired about his children, and several mentioned gifts he had purchased or made for them. He beseeched his wife to take them away from Ellicott City into the country, where they may avoid any diseases. Distraught after one of his children died of disease, Andrew permanently moved his family to Pennsylvania in 1800.[8] Andrew's preoccupation with his family and his assurances of love conveyed — or, at least, pointed to — a highly emotional, affectionate relationship between this Ellicott father and his children.

Certainly, existing letters from Joseph and Andrew revealed loving marriages and intimate families during the late eighteenth century. Yet, affection did not always bring with it a respect for the wife's intellect and a sharing of the family decision making. Recent research in family history has concluded that in the early nineteenth century the ideal of companionate marriages began to replace the instrumental marriages of the eighteenth century; instead of bonds of duty and pressure from the community, bonds of mutual affection united spouses. Ideally, a companionate marriage was a partnership based on love and respect. Joint decision making and shared activities replaced male command. This increase in status and autonomy improved conditions for wives. Unfortunately, companionate marriages also had negative repercussions and limitations. The greater expectations accompanying love often produced hurt and disillusion-ment. Most important, the amount of respect and control husbands gave their wives determined the success of the companionate marriage. With men still exercising legal and political control, companionate marriages only existed if men allowed them.[9]

Excerpts from Andrew's letters conveyed his respect for Sarah, as well as his affection for her:

> I am, my dear Sally, neither flattering you, nor myself, when I declare that, in my opinion, you are the 1st *Lady* of all my acquaintance.[10]

According to his letters, Andrew praised her "Mind and Conversation," delighted in her company, and trusted her to make most major family decisions in his absence. These references and instances suggested that he admired Sarah's intelligence and character, and held her in the highest esteem.

Various references indicate that other Ellicott men recognized their wives' intellect. For example, Eliza-beth's obituary notice of November 29, 1853 briefly described her political familiarity, intellectual capacity, and acquaintances:

> The events and Chiefs of our Revolution were familiar to her; she had exulted in the peace of 1783; she had talked with Washington, Franklin, Jefferson, Adams, Madison and Rush; her vigorous mind, improved by care-ful and continual reading, made her fit company even for them. She was a sincere and ardent lover of her country and its institutions, and had travelled over a great portion of its territory; she loved to speak of its beautiful scenery, its happy liberty, and its future prosperity.[11]

For her to have met and spoken with political leaders, Elizabeth probably served as her husband George's respected and faithful companion and confidante.

Similarly, Andrew Ellicott trusted his wife with mat-ters of great importance. In addition to expressing his respect for Sarah, Andrew's actions accorded with his words. He shared family responsibilities with her. With

Andrew frequently absent, Sarah made the family's economic decisions. After enclosing money, Andrew would stipulate a few payments to be made or clothes he needed. Otherwise, he urged Sarah to "attend to (her) necessities and wont nothing — I trust that all wise being to whose care I have so often submitted myself."[12] Since Andrew entrusted Sarah, not a male relative or friend, with the economic decisions, he granted his wife economic responsibility — a rare occurrence at the time.

Based upon the two families whose eighteenth-century letters have survived, the Ellicott marriages appeared affectionate, possibly even nascent forms of companionate marriages. Like their innovative approaches to science and education, the companionate marriage between Andrew and Sarah reflected relatively rare views for their time.[13] These, coupled with the Quaker views about spiritual love and the sanctity of the family, explained the Ellicotts' more advanced attitudes towards women and children at the turn of the century.

I

Beyond correspondence, other primary documents and records require a bit more interpretation. Family historians are often plagued with a paucity of records. Historian John Demos noted correctly that "most investigations of family life in the fairly distant past are bedeviled by one fundamental circumstance: the subject is something which the people of the time took so much for granted that it seemed to require little formal comment."[14] In fact, the most complete picture of Ellicott family life possible requires a wide variety of sources: homes, inventories, Quaker minutes, and wills.

A description of the structural layout of typical Ellicott households conveys their daily tasks and degree of privacy. Having an image of their homes affords the opportunity to place all of their daily activities and their interaction within a context. Only descriptions of the Jonathan Ellicott and the George Ellicott houses are

John Ellicott's House,
built 1772.

Jonathan Ellicott's House,
built 1782.

George Ellicott's House,
built 1789.

available. Constructed at the foot of Main Street, these two granite structures marked the location of Ellicott's Lower Mills.

Jonathan, the eldest son of Andrew and Elizabeth, built his home close to the Patapsco River Bridge in 1782, at the age of twenty-six.[15] According to a family history, the house was "of a plain and substantial character, built in accordance with the simplicity of the Friends."[16] Although a detailed description of the interior is not available, it is interesting to note that "the first-floor windows have twenty-four panes, the second floor, eighteen, and the third, twelve."[17] This simple and fairly small home housed Jonathan and his wife, Sarah, until their deaths, as well as their twelve children. Despite their large family, Jonathan encouraged guests and was a gracious host to all the visitors who filled his rooms.[18]

Across the mill-race stood his brother's home. The George Ellicott house, twice the size of Jonathan's house, is one of the few Ellicott buildings to have survived the various floods of the region — albeit in exterior shell only.[19] Built in 1789 along the Frederick Road that George surveyed as a young man, this house has long served as a model of similar Ellicott households.[20]

Originally, the house consisted of two sections: the main two and one-half story rectangular section and an attached one and one-half story kitchen ell.[21] The main part of the house was typical of its period:

> The first floor (consisted of) a central entry and stair hall, with living room and dining room to either side. On the second floor, the main chamber (was) located on the south side of the stair hall, . . . while the north side was divided into two rooms, only one of which would have been heated. A seven foot deep room was located in the front section (west side) of the second floor stair hall. The third floor or attic contain(ed) a low, sloped ceiling space with dormer on either side of the stair hall, and a storage closet beneath the eaves.[22]

Connected perpendicularly to the southeast corner of the main section both by a door and by a staircase from the basement, the kitchen addition had a large one room kitchen with a broad fireplace along the far wall, and an attic above.[23]

Roughly ten years after constructing the main and kitchen sections, George built a smaller, detached two and one-half story structure to the north and east of the house.[24] This two-bayed building served as a separate structure, probably for George Ellicott's mother or mother-in-law.[25] It had one heated room on each floor, connected by a pitched roof stair along the west wall, and a basement and dormered attic.[26]

George Ellicott   **Elizabeth Ellicott**

The house was built from locally quarried granite, layed in a coursed rubble pattern, except for the brick chimneys.[27] Wood shingles originally covered the gable roofs. Like the interior, the facade represents its period well:

> The five-bayed west facade of the main house is an elevational treatment commonly employed throughout the eighteenth century, while the relative simplicity and symmetry combined with the end chimneys are characteristics of the Federal period (1790-1820).[28]

Compared to other colonial homes, the number of bedrooms allowed for some privacy. According to Nancy

Cott's study of eighteenth-century families in Massachusetts, "privacy within the family and household as we know it — the privacy that relies on insulated walls, anonymity in a mass society, and the usual belief that what goes on in a family group is and should remain 'their own business' — simply did not prevail."[29] Within George's household, the three bedrooms and attic space could provide quite a bit of privacy during the warm months. In the winter cold, the immediate family reduced their living space, and necessarily their amount of privacy. Although the original wall thickness was not reported, the second floor original doors were one inch thick.[30] These fairly thick doors and the number of bedrooms indicated some emphasis on privacy. Furthermore, the construction of a separate structure to house an elder family member implied a sense of duty to elder family members, as well as a respect for privacy — both hers and the immediate family's.

II

Inventories, listing all of a deceased person's possessions, provided yet another description of the Ellicott household and lifestyle.[31] More than other existing records, these revealed some of the Ellicotts' daily lives' most minute details: attire, cooking, and books, to name a few. The lists were extensive, and the clues were rich. By computing the proportion of the total household value spent in different categories, two general trends emerged over the late eighteenth century and the early nineteenth century.

First, an increasing percentage of the household value was invested in business by the middle of the nineteenth century. Although the Ellicotts were businessmen from the onset, they invested more heavily in commercial ventures during the first half of the nineteenth century. The Ellicotts inventoried increased their commercial investments from about 65 (1800-1815) to nearly 92 percent (1831-1845) of the total estimated value of the estates.[32] They had owned the land that developed into Ellicott City; as the Ellicott family and Ellicott Mills grew, individual landholdings became smaller. Proceeds from the sale of land were invested in business ventures. The industrialization of the country, coupled with the scarcity of land in town, caused this shift in investments.

Second, the Ellicotts spent an increasing percentage of their expenditures on the kitchen and its appliances. Their kitchen expenditures increased from 11.7 (1800-1815) to 18.5 percent (1831-1845) of their household expenditures.[33] Although this shift was not a large one, it was a detectable one. It may have indicated a shift in values. Since the kitchen was in the women's sphere of influence, this change had important ramifications for women. Possibly, they had more economic control or a larger voice in the economic decisions. If this were the case, it points, again, to companionate marriages between the Ellicott spouses. Even if the women did not share in the economic decisions, the increase in expenditures seemed to place a greater value upon their role and position in the household. Since the kitchen equipment received more revenue (relative to bedding, tables, chairs, etc.), the women's position apparently increased in significance during this time.

Although women seemed to improve their status in the household, this information remains inconclusive. It

TABLE 1

Classification by Periods

Period	Investment	Kitchen Expenditures
	(% Invested of Total Estate Value)	(% Invested in Kitchen of Total Value of Household Expenditures)
1800-15	65.51	11.69
1816-30	81.3	14.11
1831-45	91.82	18.46

does not determine the intention of this shift — to expand the women's role in their sphere or to confine it. This could be deemed a positive change. Women would continue with their primary responsibilities, but these adopted a new cast; now, they received greater value and were considered to be more significant. On the other hand, another interpretation denounces the confinement. Women, now assigned to this role, could have been restricted to it. Significance in one particular sphere could have barred women from other ones. However, the kitchen received more revenue; this indicates that women began to be, at least, more appreciated.

Like the separation of the sexes in school, the demarcation of the spheres of influence within the household mirrored the prevalent attitudes of the time. The attitudes of the time, such as those described by the Cult of True Womanhood, led to further insulation and glorification of women, the preservers of society's moral sanctity. By describing the home as the "woman's sphere," the Cult of True Womanhood not only demarcated, but separated the spheres assigned to each sex. Apparently, the Ellicotts lived according to the dictates of this emerging ideology.

III

Just as the family allocated more resources to the Ellicott women while the men were alive, they allocated more to the women after their death. Joseph Ellicott's will of 1780 demonstrated traditional common law practice. To his "loving wife Judith," he "left one third Part of all of (his) real Estate during her natural life;"[34] in other words, she received only her due by common law, as codified by the Statute of Distributions of 1671.[35] For his children, he divided his estate:

> I do hereby Give Devise and Bequeath all my real Estate to be equally Divided share and Share alike amongst all my sons . . . they paying unto my Daughters . . . Each half as much as what each of their shares may be.[36]

The wills of the 1820's, by comparison, treated women with more economic consideration. James Ellicott's (1772-1820) will awarded his "dear mother Esther Ellicott during her natural life the sum of $1,000.00 per annum."[37] James bequeathed the remainder of his estate to his only child, Charles Ellicott. In case of Charles' death before the age of maturity (which occurred), James stipulated his Estate would "be equally divided between (his) brothers and Sisters."[38] Similarly, Andrew Ellicott's (1775-1823) will gave money to three female relatives and then divided the remainder of his estate "in equal proportions" among his three daughters and one son.[39] Upon reaching the age of 25, his daughters were "to be paid by the said Trustees . . . and (their inheritances) be then placed at their own separate control not subject however to that of their husbands should they or either of them contract matrimony."[40]

Both of these wills conveyed more egalitarian, as well as practical, attitudes not as visible in Joseph's earlier will. Economic allowances or gifts to female relatives appeared more frequently. Possibly, the Ellicott males needed to make the Ellicott women more economically secure because this generation had more children moving out of the area. No longer could the males assume that nearby relatives would be willing and financially able to care for older, dependent women.

The creation of separate estates was particularly noteworthy. Normally, a woman experienced "civil death" upon matrimony; a married woman had neither legal nor economic power. A separate estate, on the other hand, gave a woman legal control over property, thus preventing her husband — or her husband's creditors — from exercising any control over it. In this way, women could maintain financial autonomy or shield their family's holdings from "the chances and dangers of commerce" and "the casualties and hazards of Trade."[41] In addition, economic security enabled women, if they chose, not to marry. And if they chose to marry, they need not fear "civil death" or their husbands' creditors.

If separate estates gave some Ellicott women more freedom of choice, their marriage patterns confirmed it. The percentage of Ellicott women who married declined; those born from 1750-1775 had a 93 percent likelihood of marrying while those born after 1825 had a 78 percent likelihood of marrying. In addition, the average age of marriage also increased over this period. On the average, Ellicott women married roughly one year after their contemporaries did marry, but they married on par with other Quaker women.[42]

The discovery of separate estates among the Ellicotts is significant. According to historian Suzanne Lebsock, most separate estates of this period protected economic holdings from the vicissitudes of the industrial economy. By placing some of the family's land holdings in the wife's name, the family could protect it from the husband's creditors. Living husbands established many separate estates to retain family ownership of land, not to convey property or money as an inheritance. Ellicott husbands, however, may have had different motivations. The fairly prosperous Ellicotts might have bequeathed separate estate inheritances to make females more independent and to protect them from future husbands and from husbands' errors.

While still exhibiting protective attitudes towards women, later wills selected particular family members for their inheritances. Notably, in the only female will extant, most of the estate is left to women in the form of separate estates. In her will of June 4, 1842, Mary Ellicott left her estate to her "mother Mary E. Janney and her children (one daughter and one son remaining alive), and to (her) aunt Mary M. Ellicott and her daughters to be equally divided between them and held for their own exclusive and proper use and for no other use."[43]

John A. Ellicott's will of June 19, 1847, was even more selective. He bequeathed all of his estate to his son Edward T. Ellicott, who made payments to his wife and to his other children:

> Subject nevertheless to the payment of my wife Mary S. Ellicott, during her natural life, of the sum $700 per annum . . . and said annuity to be taken by her in lieu of all other claim upon my Estate Whether of dower or distributive share . . . and subject also to the payment of my son Joseph P. Ellicott, and my daughter Francis A. Henry each of the sum of $100 in cash.[44]

Possibly, industrial and commercial investments prompted these inheritance "payments." Since John had most of his investments in the iron business, it was easier to select Edward to receive his estate (consisting largely of interest in the iron business) and for Edward to make payments. This permitted the business to continue "without interruption."[45]

Evidently, the inheritance patterns of the Ellicotts' wills revealed yet another example of changing perceptions and more autonomy for women. Before the turn of the century, Joseph equally divided his estate between his sons while his daughters received lesser shares. During the 1820's, sons and daughters received equal shares, and the daughters received the protection and independence of separate estates. By the 1840's, some female protection persisted and greater selectivity appeared.

IV

The Ellicotts' marriages, household expenditures, and inheritance patterns reflect both the cultural and economic changes of the period and the Ellicott family's altered views of women and of the family. First, marriage and parental relationships, both apparently based on affection and love, typified the increasing emphasis on families and on emotions during the early nineteenth century. Second, the center of women's activity in the home received more revenue. Third, family members began to recognize and to protect women more in their wills. In these ways, the Ellicott family's lifestyle began to contribute to and to abide by a new ideology, the Cult of True Womanhood, that re-defined the women's purpose and importance in the ideal American family.

By establishing the pure and moral home as women's sphere, this ideology protected them, as well as the children they raised, from the perceived perniciousness and turpitude of the new industrial society. With the greater fluidity of society and the loss of economic security accompanying commercial investments, women needed financial security and protection. For these reasons, the wills adopted a paternalistic tone; men protected the pure, dependent women from the ravages of society and the vicissitudes of the economy. In addition to protecting women from society in general, the wills surprisingly left them more independent than before; separate estates protected them from future husbands that might exploit the womens' economic and legal dependency.

The Ellicotts' Quaker background made them receptive to, or already adhering to, many of the early nineteenth-century attitudinal changes. The Cult of True Womanhood's emphases on the sanctity of the home, respect for women, and female education accorded well with the Quaker religious principles. Since the Ellicotts, as Quakers, advocated respect for women and female education, they may have been among the earlier proponents of some of this emerging ideology's tenets, in their actions at least. Even if they merely reflected, rather than helped to establish, these attitudinal changes, the Ellicotts became early examples of them. Thus, this Quaker family provided an interesting microcosm which exaggerated the new attitudes towards family members and the industrializing nation's effects upon the family during the first half of the nineteenth century.

Footnotes

[1]Harry Lee Hoffman, Jr. and Charlotte Feast Hoffman, *American Family History: Fox, Ellicott, Evans* (Cockeysville, Maryland: Fox, Ellicott, Evans Fund, 1976), p. 20.

[2]Ibid., p. 26.

[3]Silvio A. Bedini, "Andrew Ellicott, Surveyor of the Wilderness," *Surveying and Mapping*, (June 1976), p. 113.

[4]Andrew Ellicott to Sarah Ellicott, 11 September 1785 (#846), *Ellicott Papers*, Library of Congress.

[5]Ibid., 30 July 1784 (#83).

[6]Nancy Cott, "Eighteenth-Century Family and Social Life Revealed in Massachusetts Divorce Records" in *A Heritage of Her Own*, ed. Nancy F. Cott and Elizabeth Pleck, p. 112.

[7]*Ellicott Papers*, 3 October 1784 (#836).

[8]Catherine Van Cortlandt Mathews, *Andrew Ellicott: His Life and Letters* (New York: The Grafton Press, 1908).

[9]Suzanne Lebsock, *The Free Women of Petersburg: Status and Culture in a Southern Town, 1784-1860* (New York: W.W. Norton and Press, 1984), p. 17.

[10]*Ellicott Papers*, 14 December 1792 (#900).

[11]Celia M. Holland, *Ellicott City, Maryland: Mill Town, U.S.A.* (Tuxedo, Maryland: Printers II, Inc., 1970), p. 27.

[12]*Ellicott Papers*, 14 December 1792 (#900).

[13]Even the Ellicott family motto, "Sto Super Vias Antiquas" ("I Stand Above Old Ways"), reveals a forward-looking attitude.

[14]John Demos, *A Little Commonwealth: Family Life in Plymouth Colony* (London: Oxford University Press, 1970), p. ix.

[15]Holland, p. 18.

[16]Ibid., p. 19.

[17]Ibid., p. 20.

[18]Ibid., p. 19.

[19]James R. Grieves Association, Inc. et al., "The George Ellicott House: A Feasibility Study," March 1982, p. 3.

[20]Ibid., pp. 3 & 7.

[21]Ibid., p. 7.

[22]Ibid., p. 8.

[23]Ibid.

[24]Ibid., p. 7.

[25]Ibid., p. 12.

[26] Ibid.
[27] Ibid., p. 8.
[28] Ibid.
[29] Cott, p. 113.
[30] Grieves, p. 15.

[31] Although detailed and informative, inventories have several limitations. They did not include every estate of all of the deceased, underrepresenting women and providing descriptions neither complete nor consistently classified. The most noteworthy omission was land. In addition, they aggregated some possessions under ambiguous headings. Nor could they specify which items were inherited and which were purchased. Despite these considerations, inventories offer useful pictures of the Ellicott households.

Jackson Turner Main, *The Social Structure of Revolutionary America* (Princeton: Princeton University Press, 1965), pp. 288-93.

[32] See Table 1. In this analysis, commercial investments (i.e. shares of stock in businesses or roads) are called "investments." Since land was not listed, it is not included.

In these computations, two of the inventories were not considered. First, Sarah Ellicott's estate of 1840, the only woman's estate listed, did not have any investments. Obviously, her husband chose to give her household possessions instead of investments. Since there were no other women's inventories, it is not evident whether or not this was usual.

Second, John Ellicott's estate of 1821 was not considered. John Ellicott (1769-1820) had very few commercial investments (only 1.99%). It is not known exactly why more of his money was not invested. One possibility could be that he had large landholdings not shown in the inventory. Since his children's First Guardian Accounts (Baltimore County, Guardian Accounts (9/152 and 9/153)) valued his estate at $2,338.02 on December 5, 1828, this is unlikely.

Since John was supposedly the "first inventor of steamboats," his injury may provide another possible explanation. While he was attempting to perfect the steamboat on Christmas Eve, 1790, John had an accident in which he lost his arm. (*Fox, Ellicott, Evans*, p. 152) Being handicapped after this accident, he might not have been able to earn enough money to invest a great deal.

[33] See Table 1. In this classification, kitchen expenditures includes all silverware, stoves, cooking appliances, tableware, glassware, cooking and eating utensils, urns, pots, pans, and large quantities of food listed. It does not include kitchen

furniture since tables and chairs were different classifications. In this analysis, the percentage of total household expenditure, rather than the total estimated value, will be used. (Either computation produces similar results.) Again, two estates were not included.

First, Samuel Ellicott's inventory of 1843 does not have any kitchen possessions listed. Either he lived in someone's house and did not need to have any kitchen utensils, or the person recording the estate did not consider his kitchen possessions noteworthy. In any event, he is not included in the analysis.

Second, Andrew Ellicott's estate of 1823 has a very high percentage of his household expenditures invested in his kitchen. It is not known why he had such a large percentage of his estate invested in his kitchen. This Andrew Ellicott was married to Hannah Tunis Ellicott and had four children (three daughters and one son). From the information available, his kitchen expenditures can not be explained.

Despite these reservations, some relationships seem to exist. Examining the evidence by periods makes these general trends more obvious.

[34] Anne Arundel County Original Wills (TG #1/12, 1780), Maryland Hall of Records.

[35] Lois Green Carr, "Inheritance in the Colonial Chesapeake," p. 1.

[36] Anne Arundel County Original Wills.

[37] Ellicott, Benjamin v. Ellicott, Thomas, #7639, 1826.

[38] Ibid.

[39] Ellicott, Mary M., et al. v. Janney, Samuel, et al., #7655 (168/1), 1845.

[40] Ibid.

[41] Lebsock, p. 66.

[42] See Appendix II.

[43] Ellicott, Mary M., et al. v. Janney, Samuel, et al.

[44] Howard County Original Wills (WG #1,160), 24 August 1847.

[45] Ibid.

CHAPTER VI
Outward Plantations

To claim that the Ellicotts were religious Quakers may seem inconsistent with their commercial enterprises. A constant tension may have existed between the desire to live simple, Quaker lives and the desire to succeed financially and to reap the benefits of that success.

Possibly, the Ellicotts did fit the common Quaker description of the wordly, "God-fearing, money-making" Quaker.[1] Both in England and in America, diligence and frugality enabled many to prosper. Quaker prosperity led others to question their motivations:

> As to these modern Seducers, they are not Men of Arms but a herd of insignificant People, aiming rather to heap up Riches in Obscurity, than to acquire a Fame by an heroick Undertaking. They are generally Merchants and Mechanicks, and are observ'd to be very punctual in their Dealings, Men of few Words in a Bargain, modest and compos'd in their Deportment, temperate in their Lives and using great Frugality in all Things. In a Word, they are singularly Industrious, sparing no Labour or Pains to increase their Wealth.[2]

Some described "the Children of Light (to) have been so much wiser than the Children of this World, that 'tis now good Advice to look to your Pockets when you have any dealing with the Quakers."[3]

These adages apparently belied some truth for Quaker leaders mentioned this tendency and warned against some of its consequences. As George Fox, founder of the Society of Friends, cautioned, "My Friends, that are gone, and are going over to plant, and make outward plantations in America, keep your own plantations in your hearts, with the spirit and power of God, that your own vines and lilies be not hurt."[4] As their "outward plantations" prospered and their wealth increased, many Quakers feared for the "delicate plants of their inner life."[5] According to Samuel Fothergill in 1756, the American Quakers had not heeded Fox's advice:

> Their fathers came into the country, and bought large tracts of land for a trifle; their sons found large estates come into their possession, and a profession of religion which was partly national, which descended like a patrimony from their fathers, and cost as little. They settled in ease and afluence, and whilst they made the barren wilderness as a fruitful field, suffered the plantation of God to be as a field uncultivated and desert . . . A people who had thus beat their swords into plough-shares, with the bent of their spirits to the world, could not instruct their off-spring in those statutes they had themselves forgotten.[6]

Thus, this religious minority's very success in this fertile new land may have doomed its continued existence.

In any case, it is difficult to determine which motivations, religious or economic, were the primary ones. They could have been inextricably intermingled. Many Quaker philanthropy projects, schools, and reformist endeavors required economic support. A comfortable economic situation afforded many Quakers the opportunity to bring their religious intentions to fruition. For example, schools, scholarships, and public office, required adequate funding. If all Quakers had been financially destitute, their options to serve their communities would have been more limited. Further, economic success may have been viewed, as the Puritans did view it, as an indication that God was shining upon them and divinely guided their actions.

I

Perhaps economic opportunities, rather than dreams of a holy community along the banks of the Patapsco

River, motivated the Ellicotts' move. Certainly, they were considerations.

Their establishment of Ellicott Mills, and later Batavia, New York, proved to be economically advantageous. Upon arriving in Maryland, the Ellicotts wasted no time before establishing Ellicott and Company. They built several mills, a store, a warehouse, a nail factory, and a wharf. With the profits these enterprises accrued, the Ellicotts invested in the B & O Railroad, the Union Bank, and the C & O Canal. For the most part, these holdings proved profitable.

Within the family itself, economics may have played a prominent role. For example, educating and training children invested capital in them which yielded future profit for the family. A familiarity with science had fore-seeable applications in a mill community. Even ostensibly philanthropic gestures, such as laying roads to Ellicott Mills at the Ellicotts' cost, refining their neighbor's first crop of wheat for free, and donating land and granite to different religious groups to construct churches, all proved to be wise decisions; they increased the size, demand, and accessibility of the mills and of the town.

The Ellicotts reaped the benefit of their successes. Based upon the scanty tax records available from 1783 to 1855, the Ellicotts did improve their lot.[7] Even so, the Ellicotts "died of very moderate fortunes."[8] Jonathan Ellicott, the wealthiest of the Ellicotts, was the only one to leave a "large estate."[9]

The Ellicotts' generosity provided one explanation for their "moderate fortunes," despite their numerous thriving businesses and investments. In support of religious toleration, they donated land and stone for any religious denominations in Ellicott City to build churches for their services. In addition, the Ellicotts financially assisted any school constructed in the city, as well as additional roads or other means of transportation. By 1850, Ellicott City had the Patapsco Female Institute, Rock Hill College, St. Paul's Catholic Church, Emory Methodist Church, Quaker Hill Meetinghouse, and the

B&O Railroad Station, 1857

St. Paul's Catholic Church
with
Rock Hill College above

Emory
Methodist Church

first stop of the Baltimore and Ohio Railroad.[10] Certainly, the Ellicotts actively supported the academic and religious education of their community.

II

As historian Frederick B. Tolles explains, "economic and religious considerations (were inextricably intermingled) in the complex of motives which impelled Quakers to seek new homes."[11] "The Children of Light felt that they were called to suffer for the vindication of the Truth, but they knew that an equally binding injunction was laid upon them to labor diligently in their callings for the honor of God and the welfare of their fellow men."[12]

The Ellicotts' commercial success, progressive attitudes toward business and improvements, and establishments of schools and churches expressed their "diligence" and their commitment to "the welfare of their fellow men." William Penn described Quakers as the type of persons "not only fit for, but necessary in Plantations . . . that is, Men of universal spirits, that have an eye to the Good of Posterity, and that both understand and delight to promote good Discipline and just Government among a plain and well-intending people."[13] Without doubt, Penn's words inspired the Ellicotts' actions.

Footnotes

[1]Frederick B. Tolles, *Meetinghouse and Countinghouse; The Quaker Merchants of Colonial Philadelphia, 1682-1763* (Chapel Hill: University of North Carolina Press, 1948), p. viii.

[2]Ibid., p. 47.

[3]Ibid., pp. 47-8.

[4]Ibid., p. 3.

[5]Ibid.

[6]Ibid., p. 7.

[7]Anne Arundel County and Baltimore Tax Records, Maryland Hall of Records, Annapolis, Maryland.

[8]Celia M. Holland, *Ellicott City, Maryland: Mill Town, U.S.A.* (Tuxedo, Maryland: Printers II, Inc., 1970), p. 20.

[9]Ibid.

[10]Ibid., p. 5.

[11]Tolles, p. 37.

[12]Ibid.

[13]Ibid., p. 44.

CHAPTER VII
The Ellicotts – A Quaker Family

The Quaker religion helps to explain the Ellicotts' attitudes toward the family (women and children in particular), toward education, toward public service, and toward enterprise. Their Quaker attitudes differed significantly from the attitudes of most early American families. Some of the differences resembled manifestations of attitudinal changes in the early nineteenth century. Such similarities made Quakers seem more modern or more accepting of these changes.

Since each Quaker had an "inner light," any person, regardless of sex or age, could experience spiritual rebirth. For example, belief in the new Divine Light reduced some former theological restrictions placed on women.[1] Since women could be prophets and ministers, Quaker women had more opportunities and received more respect within the faith than did many other women.[2] For example, several of the Ellicott women served in this capacity; Martha Ellicott Tyson was an Elder in the Quaker church. Her memorial, presented in a Baltimore Monthly Meeting of Friends in September, 1874, "bore testimony of her interest and convictions in Friends' principles, and of her being often called into the services of their meetings, and being eminently faithful in the performance of them."[3]

Needless to say, this view of women had important ramifications for the treatment of all women — inside and outside of the home. A greater respect for women enabled the Ellicotts to be receptive to, or possibly to help lead, important changes toward women and marriage. Since they respected women as spiritual equals and believed in romantic love before marriage, Quakers seemed to esteem and to appreciate their wives. These marriages, based more upon respect and affection than most were during the time, may have resembled the companionate marriages of the early nineteenth century — even though they resulted from religious rather than from purely romanticized, emotional reasons.

Similarly, a belief in youthful innocence led Quakers to sentimentalize and glorify children before many of their contemporaries did. Again, religious perceptions of children, more than Revolutionary theory, produced this attitude. Because the future of their meeting and of their religion hinged upon the conversion of children, the children received great care and attention — both in the form of discipline and affection.

Carefully monitored Quaker education, the "Stamp" of the parents, served a vital role. In addition to shaping future Quakers, schools protected the children from the temptations and evil of the rest of society. Here, Quakers could teach their children useful knowledge, with an emphasis on mechanical and practical things.

Like many other Quakers, the Ellicotts created their own early school. A public school open to Indian children fit Thomas Budd's plan of Quaker educational reform. In Budd's 1685 pamphlet "Good Order Established in Pennsylvania and New Jersey," he proposed that "the poor (and the Indians) receive free training in a curriculum consisting of an amalgam of practical and traditional subjects."[4] Though it is difficult to determine how many Quaker schools complied with Budd's suggestions, the Ellicotts' school certainly exemplified his Quaker ideals.

I

Like many of the Ellicotts' other characteristics, their affinity for invention and science may be a product of Quakerism. According to Quaker historian Frederick B. Tolles, "there was an intimate connection between the religious ethos characteristics of Quakerism and the demonstrable aptitude of Friends for scientific pursuits."[5] By emphasizing "concrete and material things, of actually

72

expending energy in the pursuit of truth," Quaker education inculcated a desire and an aptitude to scientifically study the world, in order to better understand God.[6] According to Tolles' theory, the Ellicotts' pursuit of scientific studies was a typical form of Quaker recreation.

II

Quaker historian Rufus M. Jones has stated that the Society of Friends tends to have two types of members. One group is committed to the ideal principles and beliefs to the degree of surrendering all possessions. The other found it "equally important to work out their principles of life in the complex affairs of the community and state, where to gain an end one must yield something; where to get on one must submit to existing conditions; and where to achieve ultimate triumph one must risk his ideals to the tender mercies of a world not yet ripe for them."[7] The latter group of Quakers described the Ellicott family.

Since books and experiments were the Ellicotts' recreation, they became intelligent and productive members of their community. They were industrious out of a love for God and creative, perhaps due to God's inspiration. Fueled by the confidence of knowing God loved them, they made a mark on the world around them.

The Ellicotts hoped for progress, education, toleration, and realization of their religious principles and beliefs; to achieve these ends, they were firmly committed to action. Entering virgin forests, they hoped to establish communities in Ellicott Mills and later Batavia based upon their beliefs. In both of these places, they were rooted in their community — a community which began in Ellicott City and expanded into other areas. With this belief in the capacity to do good and to bring about change through action, the Ellicotts typified active Quakers; they became public servants and commercial leaders, as well as marital and educational role models, in ways which suited their times and needs.

Footnotes

[1]Mary Maples Dunn, "Women of Light", p. 17.

[2]Ibid., p. 19.

[3]Harry Lee Hoffman, Jr. and Charlotte Feast Hoffman, *Fox, Ellicott, Evans: American Family History* (Cockeysville, Md.: Fox, Ellicott, Evans Fund, 1976), p. 73.

[4]J. William Frost, *The Quaker Family in Colonial America: A Portrait of the Society of Friends* (New York: St. Marten's Press, 1973), p. 95.

[5]Frederick B. Tolles, *Meetinghouse and Countinghouse; The Quaker Merchants of Colonial Philadelphia, 1682-1763* (Chapel Hill: University of North Carolina Press, 1948), p. 206.

[6]Ibid., p. 207.

[7]Ibid., p. vii.

APPENDIX I
The Ellicott Women:
A Quaker Family's Marriage Patterns

Astudy of the Ellicott women's marriage patterns had a threefold purpose. First, a comparison of the probability of marriage and the average age of marriage between this Quaker family and other contemporary families revealed how typical or atypical these women were in the context of their period. Noteworthy differences may have indicated unusual perceptions of women and of marriage. Second, changes in marriage patterns could be detected from the late eighteenth century to the early nineteenth century. Trends may have corresponded to attitudinal changes during this period.

First, the probability of marriage among Ellicott women was compared over different time periods.

Year of Birth	% Married
1750-1775	92.86
1776-1800	76.67
1801-1825	77.94

These percentages revealed some interesting trends. Women raised during the fifty year span during and following the American Revolution were less likely to marry. Various theories may explain this sharp decline in the probability of marriage. Possibly, perceptions of both women and marriage changed. For women born before 1775, marriage was a virtual necessity for economic and survival reasons. The high mortality rate before 1766 and the amount of work needed for survival caused communities to encourage marriage and children. In addition, the preponderance of men increased the chances of marriage for the available women.

After 1750, the mortality rate declined. The environment became less harsh. Alternative means of survival, such as teaching or nursing, became more viable options as some towns grew. Furthermore, the emerging revolutionary ideology and its rhetoric supported independence; certainly, some women could see the parallel. Women born after 1800 showed a slightly increased probability of marriage compared to the previous period. Possibly, these were visible results of the emergence of the Cult of True Womanhood and its celebration of marriage.

Second, comparative data provided insight into understanding changes over time. J. William Frost cited marriage statistics and the average age of marriage for American families and for Quaker families in *The Quaker Family in Colonial America*. In *Fox, Ellicott, Evans: American Family History*, Harry Lee Hoffman and Charlotte Feast Hoffman compiled genealogical information on the Ellicott family. These sources yielded the information needed to compile the following table:

Average Age of Women at Marriage

Year of Birth	Ellicott Age	Average Age	Quaker Average Age
1700- 1780	22.1	20.5	22.8
After 1780	25.3	22	24.3

Thus, the Ellicott women married at a later age than did their contemporaries. Their age of marriage seemed more typical of the average age of marrying Quaker women. Possibly, the Ellicotts, and other Quaker women, postponed marriage because Quaker communities accepted unmarried women more than other American communities did. Also, the restraint and close supervision common among Quakers reduced the chances of moral transgressions necessitating very early marriages.

According to this information, the average Ellicott women married later than did contemporary American women. Also, they were less likely to marry if raised during the years during and following the revolution. Their marriage patterns resembled those of contemporary Quaker women.

George Ellicott House

Restoration Completed 1991

George Ellicott House

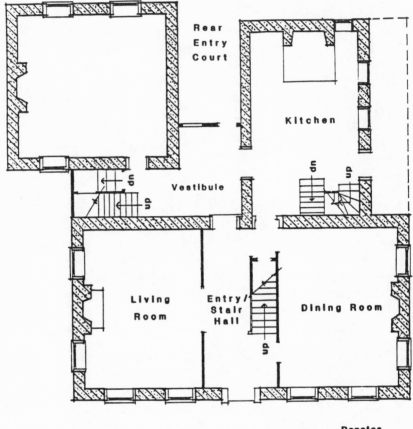

Rear
Entry
Court

Kitchen

Vestibule

up

up

up

up

Living
Room

Entry/
Stair
Hall

Dining Room

up

Denotes
Stone Walls

Floor Plan — First Floor

George Ellicott House

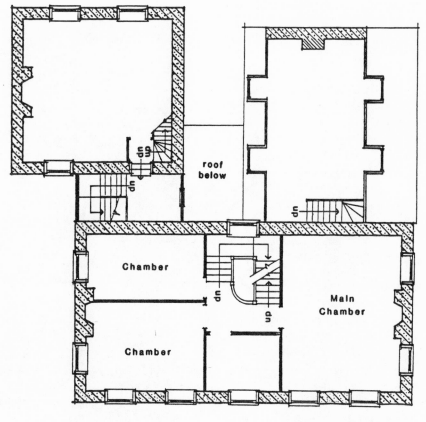

roof
below

Chamber

Main
Chamber

Chamber

Denotes
Stone Walls

Floor Plan — Second Floor

Pictures of inside of
George Ellicott House

Living Room — 1991 Restoration

Pictures of inside of George Ellicott House restored

Bibliography

"An Unusual History of the Ellicotts," *Baltimore Sun,* 8 July 1976, Enoch Pratt Library, Maryland Room, Vertical File.

Baltimore Yearly Meeting of Friends, 1760-1870. Maryland Hall of Records.

Bedini, Silvio A. "Andrew Ellicott, Surveyor of the Wilderness." *Surveying and Mapping,* June 1976.

Bedini, Silvio A. National Museum of American History, Smithsonian Institution. Interview, 7 February 1986.

Bedini, Silvio A. Personal Letter, 10 October 1986.

Bedini, Silvio A. *The Life of Benjamin Banneker.* New York: Charles Scribner's Sons, 1972, p. 73.

Bounds, Enalee E., Ellicott's Country Store. Interview, 9 January 1986.

Byrd Library, Syracuse University. Special Collections and Manuscripts. *Spaulding-Ellicott Papers.*

Carr, Lois Green. "Inheritance in the Colonial Chesapeake."

Clark, Judge John L. Marriottsville, Maryland. Interview, 9 January 1986.

Cott, Nancy F. "Eighteenth-Century Family and Social Life Revealed in Massachusetts Divorce." In *A Heritage of Her Own,* pp. 107-135, pp. 222-245.

Demos, John. *A Little Commonwealth: Family Life in Plymouth Colony.* London: Oxford University Press, 1970.

Dunn, Mary Maples. "Women of Light." In *Women of America: A History,* edited by Ruth Berkin and Mary Beth Norton. Boston: Houghton Mifflin Co., 1979, pp. 115-133.

Ellicott, Benjamin v. Ellicott, Thomas, #7639, 1826.

Ellicott, Mary M., et al. v. Janney, Samuel, et al., #7635, (168/1), 1845.

Frost, J. William. *The Quaker Family in Colonial America: A Portrait of the Society of Friends.* New York: St. Marten's Press, 1973.

Grieves, James R., Association, Inc. et al. "The George Ellicott House: a Feasibility Study," March 1982.

Heritage, September 1986, 13:3.

Hoffman, Harry Lee Jr. and Charlotte Feast Hoffman. *Fox, Ellicott, Evans: American Family History*. Cockeysville, Md.: Fox, Ellicott, Evans Fund, 1976.

Holland, Celia M. *Ellicott City, Maryland: Mill Town, U.S.A.* Tuxedo, Md.: Printers II, Inc., 1970.

Jackson, Phoebe. *Quaker Records*. Annapolis, Maryland: Maryland Hall of Records, 1974.

Kett, Joseph F. and McClung, Patricia A. "Book Culture in Post-Revolutionary Virginia." In *Proceedings of the American Antiquarian Society*, April 8, 1984, pp. 97-147.

Lebsock, Suzanne. *The Free Women of Petersburg: Status and Culture in a Southern Town, 1784-1860*. New York: W.W. Norton & Company, 1984.

Library of Congress. Manuscripts Division. *Andrew Ellicott Papers*.

Main, Gloria B. "Probate Records as a Source for Early American History." *William and Mary Quarterly*. 3rd Ser., 32 (1975), p. 98.

Main, Jackson T. *The Social Structure of Revolutionary America*. Princeton: Princeton University Press, 1965.

Maryland Hall of Records. *Anne Arundel County Original Wills*. TG #1/12, 1780.

Maryland Hall of Records. *Howard County Wills*. WG #1, 160, 1847.

Maryland Hall of Records. *Register of Wills, Inventory Accounts*. Anne Arundel, Baltimore, and Howard Counties, 1800-1860.

Mathews, Catharine Van Cortlandt. *Andrew Ellicott: His Life and Letters*. New York: The Grafton Press, 1908.

Norton, Mary Beth. *Liberty's Daughters*. Boston: Little, Brown and Company, 1980.

Stein, Charles F., Jr. *Origins and History of Howard County, Md.* Baltimore: Howard County Historical Society, 1972.

Tolles, Frederick B. *Meetinghouse and Countinghouse; The Quaker Merchants of Colonial Philadelphia, 1682-1763*. Chapel Hill: University of North Carolina Press, 1948.

Vertical File, Maryland Room. Enoch Pratt Library, Baltimore, Maryland.